Witness to History

September 11, 2001

Brendan January

Heinemann Library
Chicago, Illinois

Designed by Heinemann Library
Originated by Ambassador Litho Ltd
Printed and bound in China by
South China Printing

07 06 05 04 03
10 9 8 7 6 5 4 3 2 1

**Library of Congress Cataloging-in-Publication
Data**

January, Brendan, 1972-
   September 11, 2001 / Brendan January.
      v. cm. -- (Witness to history)
Includes bibliographical references and index.
Contents: The day the world changed -- How do we
know? -- September 11, 2001 -- The North Tower is hit
-- The Second Tower is struck -- At the center of it all
-- Explosion at the Pentagon -- Chaos at the Towers --
The first tower collapses -- Struggle aboard flight 93 --
The second tower collapes -- The United States reacts
-- The man for the moment --Fighting the fire at the
Pentagon -- The President returns to Washington
-- Rescue efforts -- A historic documentary -- Stranded
-- Bush addresses the nation -- The following days --
Worldwide reaction -- The plot -- The war against
terror -- A changed world -- Timeline -- Sources
for further research -- List of primary sources.
   ISBN 1-4034-0970-6 (HC-library binding) -- ISBN 1-
4034-3639-8 (PB)
   1. September 11 Terrorist Attacks, 2001--Juvenile
literature. [1.
September 11 Terrorist Attacks, 2001.] I. Title. II.
Witness to history
(Heinemann Library (Firm))
   HV6432.7.J36 2003
   973.931--dc21
                                    2003010628

Acknowledgments
The author and publishers are grateful to the
following for permission to reproduce copyright
material:

pp. 4-5 Hubert Boes/DPA; pp. 6, 46 AP Wide World
Photo; pp. 8, 55 Corbis; pp. 11, 25 Peter C. Brandt/Getty
Images; p. 12 Robert Clark/Aurora Photos; p. 15 Doug
Mills/AP Wide World Photo; pp. 17, 51 Reuters/Corbis;
p. 18 John Labriola/AP Wide World Photo; p. 20 Amy
Sancetta/AP Wide World Photo; pp. 23, 29, 44, 48
AFP/Corbis; p. 27 Ed Reinke/AP Wide World Photo; p.
28 Andrea Mohin/New York Times; p. 30 Don S.
Montgomery/Corbis; p. 31 Alex Wong/Getty Images; p.
32 Bettmann/Corbis; p. 35 Neville Elder/Corbis; p. 37
(top) Piel Patrick/Gamma Presse; p. 37 (bottom)
Photofest; p. 38 Jim Mone/AP Wide World Photo; p. 40
Paul Morse/The White House; p. 43 Wally Santana/AP
Wide World Photo; p. 47 Courtesy Tamim Ansary; p. 49
BBC Photo Library.

Cover photograph of a firefighter watching the smoke
at the remains of the World Trade Center, reproduced
with permission of Mark M. Lawrence/Corbis.

Photo research by Bill Broyles

The publishers would like to thank Bob Rees, historian
and teacher, for his assistance in the preparation of
this book.

The publishers would like to thank Louise Jones for all
her help and support.

Every effort has been made to contact copyright
holders of any material reproduced in this book. Any
omissions will be rectified in subsequent printings if
notice is given to the publishers.

Disclaimer
All Internet addresses (URLs) given in this book were
valid at the time of going to press. However, due to
the dynamic nature of the Internet, some addresses
may have changed, or sites may have changed or
ceased to exist since publication. While the author
and publisher regret any inconvenience this may cause
readers, no responsibility for any such changes can be
accepted by either the author or the publisher.

Some words are shown in
bold, **like this.** You can find
out what they mean by looking
in the glossary.

Contents

The Day the World Changed

On September 11, 2001, the world changed. A group of **terrorists** hijacked four passenger planes in the skies above the northeastern United States. They steered two planes into the World Trade Center in New York City. A third crashed into the Pentagon, the headquarters of the U.S. Department of Defense, outside Washington, D.C. On the fourth plane, the passengers fought back against the hijackers and the plane crashed into an empty field in western Pennsylvania.

By the end of the day, more than 3,000 people had been killed as a result of these events and the United States had declared war on terrorism.

The planners behind the attacks had selected the World Trade Center and the Pentagon for a reason. The twin towers of the World Trade Center, soaring 110 stories above the New York City skyline, were a symbol of American economic and technological power. The Pentagon, named after its distinctive shape, was the center of American military strength.

Lower Manhattan is covered in smoke after the collapse of the second tower on September 11, 2001.

"The World Trade Center is a living symbol of man's dedication to world peace," said Minoru Yamasaki, chief architect of the World Trade Center, as the towers were being built in the early 1970s.

The attackers were Muslim **extremists.** They make up only a small part of all the world's Muslims. These extremists hate Western—European and American—**culture.** They consider it immoral, and bitterly resent its popularity. They believe Muslims should be at war with the West. More than one billion Muslims live in the world today, millions of them in the United States. The vast majority of them do not share the extremists' views, and most reacted to the attacks with horror.

Most of the world did, too. In Europe and Asia, groups demonstrated in support of the United States. France's major newspaper, *Le Monde,* declared, "We are all Americans." In the United States, people lined up for hours to donate blood. Thousands of volunteers crowded into lower Manhattan in New York City to assist in the rescue efforts.

How Do We Know?

To piece together the past, historians examine primary sources—written documents, audio or video recordings, and objects.

Newspapers are excellent primary sources. They provide accounts of events as they occurred. Letters and diaries can be even more helpful. They reveal how people felt and thought as history unfolded around them. Photographs provide snapshots of people and places. Occasionally, photographs or films capture a historical event. This happened when the gigantic German airship, the *Hindenburg*, exploded in 1937, and also when U.S. President John F. Kennedy was **assassinated** in 1963.

September 11 is the most recorded event in history. This is because the attacks on the twin towers took place in New York City, the **media** capital of the world. Thousands of journalists interviewed survivors and eyewitnesses or provided their own accounts. Dozens of cameramen and onlookers recorded the second plane as it flew into the south tower. While the towers crumbled in New York City and the Pentagon burned in Washington, D.C., millions of people around the world watched on television.

The large number of these primary sources is extraordinary, but historians can also research new sources on the Internet. After the attacks, people sent millions of e-mails that detailed their feelings and reactions. In chat rooms, people from different **cultures** and nations discussed the meaning of the attacks.

Students at Penn State University gather around a large-screen television to watch the unfolding events in New York City and Washington, D.C.

"Today I awoke for the first time in my life with a real sense of fear, wondering if the government, who I rarely ever consider during the course of a day, a week or even a month, much less first thing in the morning, could protect me," wrote Linda Nuñez in an e-mail on September 14. "And while I may have been naive in my previous sense of security, it sure was nice. Today I wonder if I will ever again awaken with that kind of peace in my heart, and now know why my elder Americans have thus far looked upon me with a face of gentle envy. For they know of the wars and tragedies that befell our great nation long before I ever had to consider them. Today I consider them, as well as all the men and women who have died to offer me the precious sense of safety and freedom that I have usually taken for granted."

Historians, today and in the future, will use these primary sources to tell the story of September 11. They will seek to answer important questions such as what kind of a global community were we before the attacks, why did the attacks happen in the first place, and what have we since become.

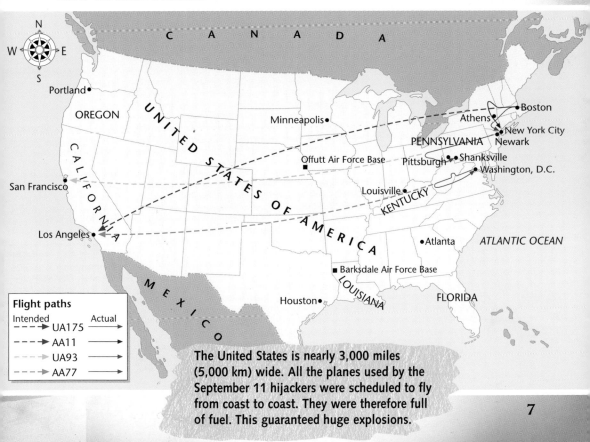

Flight paths

Intended	Actual
----> UA175	---->
----> AA11	---->
----> UA93	---->
----> AA77	---->

The United States is nearly 3,000 miles (5,000 km) wide. All the planes used by the September 11 hijackers were scheduled to fly from coast to coast. They were therefore full of fuel. This guaranteed huge explosions.

September 11, 2001

The dawn of September 11 was clear and bright over New York City and Washington, D.C. It promised to be a beautiful autumn day. There was no mist or fog, and **visibility** was excellent.

At about 8 A.M., American Airlines Flight 11 (AA11) took off from Logan International Airport in Boston. Eighty-one passengers and eleven crew were on board the plane, which was headed for Los Angeles. The air traffic controller told the pilots to turn right and climb to 35,000 feet (10,668 meters). After fourteen minutes, however, the plane was flying at only 29,000 feet (8,839 meters) and was no longer answering radio calls.

After 8:30 A.M., a phone call came from AA11 senior flight attendant Madeline Amy Sweeney. She reported that the plane had been hijacked. She said the hijackers had assaulted two flight attendants and killed a passenger. Calmly, she told the controller the hijackers' seat numbers so police could identify them and begin investigating. At about 8:46 A.M., she said she could see the Hudson River and the buildings of New York City. Then she said slowly, "Oh my God."

The World Trade Center's twin towers were a defining feature of the famous New York City skyline.

At 8:14 A.M., the air traffic controller in Boston was not receiving any contact from American Airlines Flight 11. An air traffic controller in Athens, New York, discussed the problem with him.

8:14:33, Controller A (based in Logan, Boston):
"This is Boston. I turned American 20 left and I was going to climb him. He will not respond to me now at all."

Controller B (based in Athens, New York):
"Looks like he's turning right."

Controller A: "Yeah, I turned him right."

Controller B: "Oh, O.K."

Controller A: "And he's only going to, um, I think 29 [thousand feet]."

Controller B: "Sure. That's fine."

Controller A: "Eh, but I'm not talking to him."

Controller B: "He won't answer you. He's nordo [no radio] roger. Thanks."

At 8:24:38, the controllers heard the hijackers speaking on the plane's intercom to the passengers.

"We have some planes, just stay quiet and you will be OK. We are returning to the airport. Nobody move, everything will be OK. If you try to make any moves you'll endanger yourself and the airplane. Just stay quiet."

At 8:33:59, the hijackers spoke for the last time over the intercom.

"Nobody move please. We are going back to the airport. Don't try to make any stupid moves."

9

The North Tower Is Hit

At 8:46 A.M., AA11 smashed into the north tower of the World Trade Center. Loaded with almost 11,900 gallons (45,000 liters) of jet fuel, the plane tore through ten floors and exploded in a giant fireball that scattered glass, steel, and millions of bits of paper.

The giant tower rumbled, shook, and swayed. Many who worked between the 94th and 104th floors were killed instantly. Burning jet fuel poured down the elevator shafts and blew out windows on the street level. Throughout the building, workers rushed to the nearest emergency exits. All elevators stopped. People on the top floors, some of them severely burned, would have to walk down more than 80 flights of stairs.

The north tower burned fiercely, staining the blue sky above the city with smoke. The streets around the towers were soon choked with ambulances, police cars, and fire engines. Firefighters—carrying hoses, first-aid kits, oxygen tanks, and tools—rushed into the building and began a long climb to help the **evacuation.** In the stairwells, thousands of workers formed lines and made their way down.

In the south tower, there was little sense of urgency. News spread quickly about a fire in the north tower, but no one knew the cause. An announcement came over the public address system: people could leave the building or return to their desks.

Manhattan is the heart of New York City. The World Trade Center, at the **commercial hub** of the modern Western world, was in New York's financial district in southern Manhattan.

John Labriola's account

John Labriola was on the 71st floor of the north tower when the plane struck. He joined the people streaming down the building's stairs and was safely evacuated.

The building rocked in one direction, then shuddered back and forth. It felt like it moved five or six feet [1.5 or 2 meters] in each direction. . . . People were covering their mouths against the smoke. It was very hot. We were slipping on the sweat of those who had gone before. . . . Around the 35th floor we started meeting the stream of firefighters walking up. None of them said a word. I can't stop thinking about the look in their eyes, how heroic they were. . . . We had to press into a single file so the firefighters could march past. They were carrying unbelievable loads of equipment and were already exhausted by the time we started seeing them. The people going down were very polite to one another. They helped others who needed it, and they waited for each other. One man literally carried a woman down the steps because she was unable to make it on her own. Two others helped a guy on crutches.

At the height of a normal workday, about 50,000 people occupied the World Trade Center. Because the attacks occurred early in the morning, only about 15,000 people were in the towers.

11

The Second Tower Is Struck

At 9 A.M., President George W. Bush was visiting a Florida elementary school to promote his education plan. As he entered the building, he was told that one of the twin towers of the World Trade Center was on fire after being struck by an aircraft. There were few other details. The president spoke briefly with an **aide.** He thought the pilot of the plane had probably suffered a heart attack and lost control.

At about the same time, a little more than ten minutes after the north tower was hit, flight controllers lost contact with United Airlines Flight 175, which had left Boston at 8:14 A.M. The plane was carrying 56 passengers and 6 crew members.

In New York City, more than two hundred firefighters had gathered at the north tower. Around 9 A.M., Flight 175 suddenly appeared from the southwest. It streaked over the city's harbor and angled its wings just before it crashed into the south tower. Floors 78 to 80 exploded into a huge orange-and-black fireball. The tower began to burn.

The images of a passenger airliner steering directly into the tower were shown around the world, shocking viewers and causing fear. What had seemed to be an accident was actually a deliberate attack.

This is United Airlines Flight 175, moments before it struck the south tower. The north tower is already burning.

Bob Borski's description
Bob Borski, 32, a financial director at AIG Insurance, was watching the towers from six blocks away when the second tower was hit.

It just doesn't fit into your mind—I'm used to seeing planes and helicopters disappear behind the building. And they come out the other side. But this was so low and it literally disappeared into the building. It was a swift explosion. It was boom—like a door shutting. Quick and loud.

Carl Cunneff's experience
Carl Cunneff, 36, an oil **broker,** worked near the towers.

Police guided us across the West Side Highway, then we heard a loud roar and looked to see a second jet headed right for the south tower. We heard the engines speed up as it turned sideways and hit the corner of the building head on. It looked like it melted into a fireball. We thought there might be other planes. So we all started running toward the Hudson River to the ferry service to New Jersey. The ferry was packed with people crying and hugging one another, not knowing if their coworkers were dead or alive.

Jim McMahon's recollection
Jim McMahon worked in the World Trade Center. He arrived at the scene soon after 9 A.M.

Everyone on the street, it seemed, was standing still, riveted to the scene. . . . Just then the south tower, my building, exploded with a deafening boom that rattled me, and sent me reeling. . . . It was an explosion so big, that it appeared to cut the tower in two, and the **debris** from the blown-out floors as well as the top portion that had been cut off appeared to be falling in my direction. The crowd, which had been quietly watching the fire, now found itself in the path of an exploding skyscraper. There was instant panic. . . . In unison, everyone turned to run, pushing the person in front of them in a desperate attempt to escape.

At the Center of It All

In Florida, President Bush was seated before a classroom of seven- and eight-year-olds when an **aide** walked over to him and whispered a message. "A second plane has hit the World Trade Center. America is under attack." Bush stiffened and nodded. He turned back to the class and explained that he had to leave.

Twenty minutes later, Bush appeared emotional as he spoke to television cameras. Calling the attacks a "national tragedy," he vowed that **"terrorism** against our nation will not stand."

Bush left the school and was driven to Air Force One, the president's plane. "We're at war," he told his aides. "That's what we're paid for, boys."

In Washington, D.C., air traffic controllers detected a passenger plane—American Airlines Flight 77—just 50 miles (80 kilometers) away. Some of the 64 people on board had made phone calls to report that they had been hijacked. Flight 77 was heading straight for the city.

At the White House, Vice President Dick Cheney's office door flew open. "Sir," said a secret service agent to Cheney, "we have to leave immediately." The agents grabbed Cheney, lifted him off his feet and hauled him out of the office. They took him down several flights of stairs to an underground tunnel that was connected to a **bunker.** High overhead, American Airlines Flight 77 circled the city and selected its target.

President Bush's reaction
President Bush, like most of the nation, was not physically present when the attacks occurred. In an interview with *Newsweek* magazine, he explained what was going through his mind when he heard the news.

"I was very aware of the cameras. America is under attack. I'm trying to absorb that knowledge. I have nobody to talk to. I'm sitting in the midst of a classroom with little kids, listening to a children's story . . . and I realize I'm the commander in chief and the country has just come under attack."

Minutes later, Bush left the classroom and saw recorded pictures of the plane striking the second tower.

"I was angry. I was furious. But I had also realized that I needed to be clearsighted. I needed to understand exactly what was happening, get a feel for who was doing this, and prepare to respond."

Bush, sitting in front of a classroom of 7- and 8-year-olds, hears from his chief of staff of the attack on the second tower.

Explosion at the Pentagon

At 9:39 A.M., American Airlines Flight 77 swooped over the Pentagon, the headquarters of the U.S. military, just outside Washington, D.C. The plane flew directly into the building's southwest side. This was the section that housed military staff. Like the planes that crashed in New York City, AA77 was full of jet fuel. The flames exploded down corridors and into offices, spewing smoke and blasts of hot air.

The lights went out. Dazed survivors crawled on the floor. By the light of the fires, they searched for safety around blown-out ceiling tiles and snarls of tangled wire. Farther away, city residents watched in disbelief as a dark column of smoke appeared on the horizon.

News of the disaster spread. The White House was **evacuated,** and secret service agents carrying **automatic weapons** patrolled nearby Lafayette Park. In the **bunker** deep beneath the White House, Cheney and other officials made quick decisions. All airplanes in the air above the United States—more than 4,000—were ordered to land immediately. All international flights were cancelled. George Bush and Dick Cheney spoke on the phone. If any more passenger planes were hijacked and directed toward targets, they were to be shot down by fighter planes.

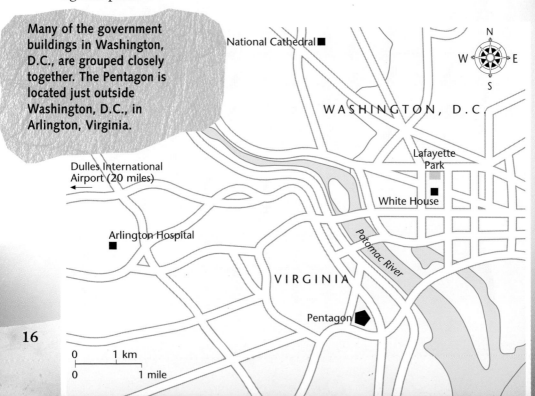

Many of the government buildings in Washington, D.C., are grouped closely together. The Pentagon is located just outside Washington, D.C., in Arlington, Virginia.

National Cathedral ■

WASHINGTON, D.C.

Lafayette Park

Dulles International Airport (20 miles)

White House

Arlington Hospital ■

VIRGINIA

Potomac River

Pentagon ⬠

0   1 km

0   1 mile

About 24,000 people occupy the Pentagon during a normal workday. Here, firefighters battle the flames at the Pentagon as a rescue helicopter surveys the damage.

The traffic was, you know, typical rush-hour—it had ground to a standstill. I looked out my window and I saw this plane, this jet, an American Airlines jet, coming. And I thought, "This doesn't add up, it's really low." And I saw it. I mean it was like a cruise missile with wings. It went right there and slammed right into the Pentagon. Huge explosion, great ball of fire, smoke started billowing out. And then it was chaos on the highway as people tried to either move around the traffic and go down, either forward or backward.

We had a lady in front of me, who was backing up and screaming, "Everybody go back, go back, they've hit the Pentagon." It was just sheer terror.

TV interview with Mike Walter
Mike Walter, of *USA Today*, was sitting in rush-hour traffic near the Pentagon when AA77 struck. He recounted what he saw during an interview with the TV news channel CNN.

Chaos at the Towers

In New York City, all airports were shut down and the bridges and tunnels leading into Manhattan were closed. The Metropolitan Museum of Art and the Empire State Building were **evacuated.**

Emergency crews and firemen rushed into both towers of the World Trade Center. The stairwells were packed with people walking down. Most were calm, but as the smoke and heat spread many panicked or fainted. Some people never left their floors. They were paralyzed with fear or confusion and unable to grasp what was happening.

Others could not get to the stairwells. In the north tower, the plane had sliced through the building and destroyed the three staircases leading down. For the 1,100 people on the higher floors of both towers, there was no hope of escape.

A firefighter waits for orders as people calmly descend the escalators in the south tower.

Al Jones's description
Throughout the city, dozens, if not hundreds, of journalists were heading to downtown Manhattan to report on the attacks. ABC News reporter Al Jones describes meeting a person who had been evacuated.

I ran into a fellow who was on the 64th floor of the north tower when the first plane hit. He said everything was orderly. They were evacuating. But when the second explosion occurred and they lost power, lost lights, it was **pandemonium**. He said they just rushed down the stairs, firefighters were there to try to lead them out. He came out dazed, covered with soot, covered with ash. Staggering away from the building, lucky to be alive.

M. Corey Goldman's experience
M. Corey Goldman, also an ABC reporter, describes on the ABC website what happened as she took an underground train to the World Trade Center.

The conductor announces that, due to an emergency, trains are being stopped. We slowly creep into the Chambers Street subway station. As I run up the stairs and emerge on to the street, I am confronted with a scene out of a horror movie: both towers, looming tall above me, both with massive fiery holes in them and smoke billowing out. The streets are filled with people, dazed and confused, wandering aimlessly.

The First Tower Collapses

Suddenly, at 9:59 A.M., the south tower abruptly collapsed. The structure—its steel supports melted like plastic by the burning jet fuel—lurched and fell. Witnesses remember hearing a deep roar. The concrete floors slammed together, one on top of another, as they crashed downward. Glass, steel, and concrete exploded, and a wall of smoke and dust poured through the streets. The crowds of people around the World Trade Center fled.

The south tower collapses in a rush of debris. A survivor likened the sound it made to "a thousand runaway trains."

The force of the collapse overturned cars, blew out windows, and crushed a nearby church. Fire engines and ambulances were smashed in the cascade of **debris.** The streets around the site were darkened in clouds of soot and dust. Survivors, their faces covered with rags, walked in a daze. Many remembered being stunned by the silence that followed. When the breeze blew away the clouds, people saw that the skyline was empty: the tower was gone.

Stephen King's experience

Stephen King, a fire battalion chief, was in the north tower when the south tower collapsed.

John Frey remembers
John Frey, a 52-year-old finance expert, describes his experiences after the second tower fell as he was leaving his workplace on Wall Street, in New York City's financial district, just southwest of the World Trade Center.

It was completely pitch black. You could not see your hands. I heard people bumping into people and falling and screaming for help. I was completely **disoriented.** I couldn't even tell which way was the sidewalk. I could see absolutely nothing. I wasn't sure if I was blind or if it [the air] was that black. My eyes were stinging so badly. My eyes were closing. Eventually a cop saw me and put me on a bus. I got off [and] went to a pharmacy to get some drops for my eyes. The cashier looked at me and started to cry.

Michelle Preli's account
Michelle Preli, a producer for MSNBC.com, reported on the scene.

The situation is chaos. The Manhattan Bridge and Brooklyn Bridge are just full of people covered in white ash. There's a huge smell of **char** in the air. People are walking with masks, with their shirts off . . . [It is] total shock.

The noise becomes deafening. I can feel the ground shaking . . . . I remember just hearing the noise. You know it's coming down and that this is it. It's all over. Absolutely got to be. I remember being under the arch [in the north tower] and saying to myself, this is a joke. I'm going under an arch. I've got 110 stories coming down [on top of me]. It's over, Steve. I literally remember that.

21

Struggle aboard Flight 93

As New York City and Washington, D.C., reeled under the attacks, another plane was hijacked by four more **terrorists.** United Airlines Flight 93, with 45 people on board, had taken off from Newark, New Jersey, at 8:42 A.M. About five minutes later, the plane began to climb without permission from air traffic controllers. Near Pittsburgh, it made a hard turn back toward Washington, D.C. (map page 7).

Calls came from the aircraft's passengers, reporting that they had been hijacked. Passenger Jeremy Glick called his wife, Lyzbeth, and asked if any planes had been flown into the World Trade Center. Lyzbeth answered yes.

> **Lisa Jefferson's phone call**
> Lisa Jefferson, a telephone company supervisor, took a call from Todd Beamer, a passenger on Flight 93.

Glick was one of four men aboard Flight 93 who spoke over the telephone about taking back control of the airplane. Todd Beamer told a telephone operator that they might rush the hijackers. Tom Burnett called his wife in California with news of the hijacking and said they were going to do something about it. Mark Bingham spoke to his mother and told her he loved her.

No one knows exactly what happened on board Flight 93. On the phone lines there were shouts, screams, and then silence. At about 10 A.M., Flight 93 crashed in a field in Shanksville, Pennsylvania, killing everyone on board.

The crash took place only 80 miles (128 kilometers) from Washington, D.C. "I think an act of heroism just took place," Vice President Cheney later said.

> They picked the wrong plane to hijack because these were "Type-A" type people generally. They . . . were not going to allow someone to force them into something they didn't want to do.
> Jere Longman, *New York Times* journalist

When I took over the call, there was a gentleman on the line, very soft spoken, calm. . . . He told me there were three people that were taking over the flight. Two of them have knives and they have locked themselves in the cockpit. One had a bomb strapped around his waist with a red belt. He told me at that point that if he didn't make it, would I please make a phone call and call his wife and his family and let them know that he loved them very much. . . . He said that, would I say the Lord's Prayer with him. And he recited the Lord's Prayer from top to bottom. . . . At that point he told me that him and a few other guys were thinking about jumping the guy with the bomb. If it didn't work, he wanted me to make a phone call and make a promise to him that I would call his wife. He turned from me to speak to someone else and he said, "Are you ready?" I couldn't hear the response. He said, "OK. Let's roll."

Investigators search the wreckage of United Airlines Flight 93, looking for evidence and the flight data recorder.

The Second Tower Collapses

In Manhattan, thousands were fleeing the city center. The south tower was gone. The north tower, still burning, could collapse at any moment.

The city's roads and bridges, usually jammed with cars, were crowded with people. Few of them knew exactly where they were heading. But they all seemed to feel that the farther away from the World Trade Center they could get, the safer they would be.

The north tower continued to burn until 10:28 A.M. Then, the top crumbled. The floors crashed downward, exploding in another cloud of dust and **debris** that rolled through the city streets. The crowds crossing the Brooklyn Bridge felt it shudder. From the Statue of Liberty, rising from the Hudson River west of the southern tip of Manhattan Island, the view of lower Manhattan was covered in smoke.

Almost 500 firefighters, police, and emergency workers disappeared in the **carnage.** Emergency radios that had crackled with messages suddenly went silent. In lower Manhattan, around the ruined World Trade Center, no blue sky could be seen. The terrible thunder of the collapsing tower gave way to darkness and silence. As Dan Rather, a **veteran** television news reporter, said, "There are no words to describe this."

Regina Wilson's description
Regina Wilson, a firefighter with Engine 219, describes the moment when the cloud from the second collapse covered her fire engine.

We completely condemn this serious operation. . . . We were completely shocked. . . . It's unbelievable, unbelievable, unbelievable.
Palestinian President Yasser Arafat

The next thing we knew, this black smoke came and pushed against us and covered us, and everything went completely black. Four of the five of us were standing in back of the engine. The boss was talking to us, saying "everybody just stay calm, stay calm, we're going to be okay." It was so dark, I couldn't see my hands in front of my face. Finally it started to clear up, and the boss started asking, "Is everybody okay?" At first, we thought one of our guys was missing, but he wound up being inside the engine.

For several days after September 11, the same images would be shown over and over again on television screens around the world: the first tower boiling with smoke, the dark outline of a plane steering into the second tower, an orange fireball, and then the towers crumbling.

The United States Reacts

The roar of jets sounded again over New York City, and some worried that yet another attack was coming. This time, however, it was a pair of fighter planes circling the city.

The shock of the attacks and the scenes of destruction were spread on television and radio, shaking the nation. People who had woken up to a beautiful September morning now realized that the country was suddenly at war.

U.S. military bases around the world were put on Delta—the highest alert. The aircraft carriers USS *John F. Kennedy* and USS *George Washington* steamed out of their ports. Along with several other warships armed to shoot down aircraft, they took up positions along the eastern coast of the United States.

George Bush was on board the presidential plane, Air Force One, which had zig-zagged over the Atlantic Ocean in order to confuse potential attackers.

Vice President Dick Cheney remained in the underground **bunker** beneath the White House, grimly watching the disaster unfold on television. **Snipers** had taken positions on the White House roof. Cheney urged Bush to stay away from Washington, D.C. Bush agreed, and Air Force One landed at the Barksdale Air Force Base in Louisiana.

Across the country, people reacted to the attacks by seeking to help. Lines quickly formed outside hospitals and blood banks.

Claudia Brown's description
Claudia Brown, 46, a spokeswoman for the Red Cross in Portland, Oregon, describes people's desire to offer help.

It's such a terrible feeling, a sense of helplessness, and giving blood is a patriotic act. It's something I can do as a citizen. You want to find out who's responsible. If I could leap up and punch someone in the face I would, but this is a more constructive way of dealing with it [the helplessness and anger].

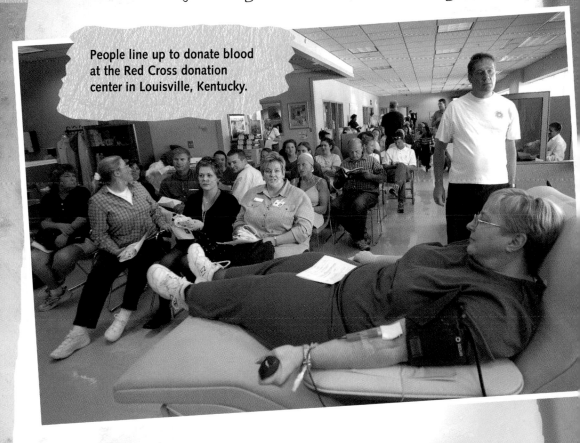

People line up to donate blood at the Red Cross donation center in Louisville, Kentucky.

I was stunned. Within two hours we had a line of donors that stretched out the front door, and cars were circling the block looking for a place to park. People are heartbroken. We're all in this together, even though we're 3,000 miles apart. I think since we weren't physically touched by this, people here feel we have a responsibility to do what we can to help.

The Man for the Moment

In Manhattan, survivors and emergency workers began searching through the smoking mounds of twisted steel and shattered concrete where the towers had once stood.

On the streets and the highways, tens of thousands of people streamed northward. Many had hair that was knotted with dust or had piles of soot on their shoulders. Lines of people formed at pay phones to call loved ones. Religious services at the city's largest churches and synagogues were filled.

The city had recently built a $15-million command center for just such disasters—but it was located in the World Trade Center. When the towers collapsed, Mayor Rudolph W. Giuliani and his **aides** were briefly trapped in the command center. They managed to escape, and opened a new post in an old firehouse. After just ten minutes, they were forced to flee again. Everyone who stayed behind was killed.

With the president in an unknown location, Giuliani became the face and voice that reassured the nation. He answered questions from reporters. He urged New Yorkers not to direct group hatred at the city's many Muslims.

"I have a sense it's a horrendous number of lives lost," said Giuliani. "Right now we have to focus on saving as many lives as possible."

A news report
Stephen Evans, a BBC reporter, described Giuliani's ability to reach out to fellow New Yorkers on September 11.

Joseph Silvester, who worked at the World Financial Center, crosses the Brooklyn Bridge after the collapse of the towers.

For the rest of the day, [Giuliani] gave a series of **impromptu** press conferences, often in streets strewn with **debris.** Of course there was nothing unusual about that—it's what politicians do at disasters—but many fail to connect with the public, missing the moment, their presence seeming like an intrusion.

By contrast, Giuliani created leadership in chaos. He shared the city's grief, but also **instilled** determination and resolution. . . . He caught the mood of his citizens, **articulating** their thoughts, shaping feelings barely formed in the public mind. He **exhorted** New Yorkers to partake of the good things of life. It was the kind of instruction that might have seemed insensitive if the Mayor hadn't known the true spirit of his city.

Mayor Giuliani toured the site of the disaster on September 12 with the governor of New York, George Pataki, and New York Senator Hillary Clinton.

Fighting the Fire at the Pentagon

Throughout the afternoon and into the evening, black, choking smoke boiled from the Pentagon's western side. Thousands were **evacuated** as emergency workers and firefighters tried to control the fire. When panic-fuelled reports came that other passenger planes were headed for the city, the firefighters were forced to take cover until an all-clear was given. When an F-16 fighter plane soared overhead, hundreds cheered.

At 10:10 A.M., a section of the Pentagon collapsed, weakened by the explosion and heat from the fire. The fire was not brought under control until later that night.

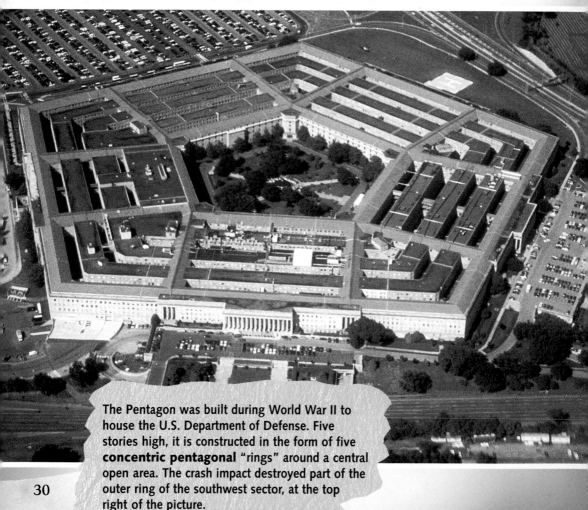

The Pentagon was built during World War II to house the U.S. Department of Defense. Five stories high, it is constructed in the form of five **concentric pentagonal** "rings" around a central open area. The crash impact destroyed part of the outer ring of the southwest sector, at the top right of the picture.

Greg Gulick's experience
Greg Gulick, a 32-year-old **veteran** of the Gulf War
(1990–1991), was a firefighter called to the Pentagon.

We knew we had a job to do. We went into the building, searching for victims. There was so much fire, smoke and damage. You couldn't see a lot because of the smoke. It was dark, black smoke, and the walls were buckled out, and fire was balling down the hallway. We did not see people inside. We were on the ground floor. I haven't felt something that hot before. We were just doing what we could. They evacuated us three times because of reports of other planes, and then the fire would gain, and there was nothing we could do but keep fighting it. I was there until 4 P.M. I got **dehydrated** and was taken to Arlington Hospital. It felt good to be home.

The plane hit the Pentagon between the ground and second floors. The FBI took charge of the site as the fire was brought under control, and firefighters and military personnel reentered the building to search for survivors.

The President Returns to Washington

By noon, Air Force One had landed at Barksdale Air Force Base in Louisiana. In the three hours since Bush had last spoken to the public, the World Trade Center towers had collapsed, the Pentagon had been attacked, and all commercial planes above the United States had been grounded.

Air Force guards—wearing helmets and bulletproof vests, and carrying rifles—surrounded Bush's plane when it stopped. Bush wanted to assure the nation and the world that the U.S. government was still functioning. He gave a brief speech of 204 words and again boarded Air Force One. The plane took off, this time travelling to Offutt Air Force Base, a high-security facility in Nebraska. No one was certain whether the **terrorists** would strike again, and the president's security advisors were concerned that the president himself was a target. Bush stayed in touch with his top advisers and with Vice President Cheney. By mid-afternoon, Bush had decided to return to Washington, D.C.

Air Force One is the name given to either of two Boeing 747s (jumbo jets) reserved for the use of the U.S. president. They have extra electronic and technical equipment, and can be refuelled during flight.

President Bush's recollections
President Bush recalled some of his first thoughts on
September 11 for CBS News.

I can remember sitting right here in this office [aboard Air
Force One] thinking about the consequences of what had taken
place and realizing it was the defining moment in the history
of the United States. I didn't need any legal briefs. I didn't
need any consultations. I knew we were at war.

CBS News, after interviewing those who had been on Air Force
One, reported on the president's concern on September 11
that he had not yet returned to Washington, D.C.

With the president out of sight, some wondered who was
running the government. Bush was not seen since the attack
on Washington, except by those aboard Air Force One. Mr
Bush worried about this—he was overheard saying, "The
American people want to know where their dang president is."

Lieutenant General Keck recalls
Lieutenant General Keck, commander of the 8th Air Force, was
at Barksdale on the morning of September 11. Around 10 A.M.,
he was told that a large, unidentified plane would be landing
at the base and would need security. Before noon, Air Force
One was on the ground and Keck was playing host to the
president of the United States.

While he was fairly angry, he was very much in control. He
already knew the response of the American people—shock,
grief, rage. He already anticipated that.

Rescue Efforts

In New York City, hundreds of firefighters and rescue workers dug frantically at the six-story pile of ruins that had once made up the twin towers of the World Trade Center. They formed bucket brigades, passing the buckets along a chain of people to remove the thick, grey dust one shovelful at a time. Rescuers strained to hear the cries of buried victims. Search dogs roamed among the wreckage, their noses pressed to the ground.

When the rescuers discovered a sign of life, they yelled for everyone to be quiet. The movement of the firefighters, like ants on a giant hill, stopped. The rescuers called for silence many times, but found only about twenty people still alive.

At some city hospitals, doctors outnumbered the injured. Ambulances pulled up empty, and nurses waited impatiently next to rows of wheelchairs. As the afternoon turned into evening, they realized that there were few injured survivors. Those who could escape had done so. The rest were dead.

> **It was the most horrific scene I've ever seen in my whole life.**
> New York City Mayor Rudolph W. Giuliani

Craig Childs' description

Around the World Trade Center site, hundreds of volunteers gathered with hopes of helping. But only emergency crews and skilled workers, such as welders, were allowed into the ruins, which was called Ground Zero. Volunteers, like Craig Childs, found a new purpose: they would cheer those entering and leaving the site.

A firefighter surveys Ground Zero. This term, which originally referred to the spot below a nuclear explosion, was used as a name for the World Trade Center ruins.

Wearing bandannas and dust masks, we applauded the streams of emergency vehicles leaving Ground Zero, we shouted out thanks and the vehicles kept coming—ambulances, troop trucks full of dusty rescuers, semi trucks loaded with huge tangles of metal and stairways and window glass. I reached out and high-fived a **paramedic** sticking her arm from the ambulance window. The workers stared at us in disbelief. Expressions of confused joy began to appear on their faces, as they honked and flashed their lights. In the other lane, a steady rush of replacement vehicles, sirens blaring, heading downtown.

When I finally walked away into the next street, faint with smoke, my hands hurt from all the clapping. If I couldn't lift wreckage and search for survivors, at least my hands were sore from supporting those who could.

A Historic Documentary

Two French filmmakers, Jules and Gédéon Naudet, made one of the most important historical records of September 11.

The two brothers had come to New York City in early summer 2001 to make a **documentary** about a young **rookie** firefighter named Tony Benetatos. Throughout the summer months, Jules and Gédéon filmed the firefighters of southern Manhattan's Engine 7, Ladder 1 unit. The fire station was situated just north of the World Trade Center.

From July to early September, nothing much happened. Tony despaired that he would ever see a fire. Early on the morning of September 11, Jules went with the firefighters to check a gas leak. As they waited outside on the pavement, the men heard the jet engines of a 767 flying low overhead. Jules pointed his camera up and photographed the only images of the first plane smashing into the north tower of the World Trade Center.

Dozens of cameramen would film the horrible pictures of the towers burning and collapsing, but only Jules captured what happened inside the towers. Through Jules's camera, we see the lines of tense firefighters waiting to climb the stairs; the chiefs trying to keep radio contact; the fire **chaplain** praying; and the dark, frantic moments after the south tower collapsed.

> **They always say that there is a witness to history, I guess that day we were chosen to be the witness.**
> Jules Naudet

Jules Naudet's thoughts
Jules Naudet filmed some of the only surviving footage of what occurred in the south tower as the attacks unfolded. He also captured the moments when the north tower collapsed right next door.

When the Naudets' documentary was screened in the United States in March 2002, 39 million people watched.

That day, you go through every range of emotion possible. Fear and terror, sadness and loss, because I thought I had lost my brother and my friends. I think it was a few days later, when I got a chance to look at the tape, I realized this was the only record of it. But with that comes a responsibility.

Stranded

Except for fighter planes, the airspace above the United States was cleared. Government officials said it would be days before flights were resumed. When they heard this news, many of the thousands trapped in the nation's airports took to the road. Businesspeople hopped on buses or trains or hitched rides. Friendships were forged on day-long trips across the country.

Other flights from overseas never reached the United States. Dozens of planes were approaching the country when the airspace was closed. They were forced to land at other airports, especially in Canada and Mexico. Long lines of planes formed on remote runways. When the news of the attacks spread, passengers were shocked. They also faced uncomfortable hours waiting in cramped planes before they could unload.

Grounded planes sit on the tarmac at Minneapolis–St. Paul Airport while U.S. airspace remains closed.

A Delta Airlines flight attendant's recollections
This flight attendant gave an account of the impact of events on her flight.

We were over the North Atlantic and I was taking a scheduled rest break. All of a sudden the curtains parted violently and I was told to go to the cockpit. As soon as I got there I noticed the crew had one of those "all business" looks on their faces. The captain handed me a printed message. The message was from Atlanta, addressed to our flight, and simply said, "All airways over the Continental US are closed." . . . We knew it was a serious situation and we needed to find [land] quickly.

We decided to lie to the passengers for the time being. We told them that an instrument problem had arisen on the plane and that we needed to land at Gander [in Canada] and have it checked. There were already 20 other planes on the ground from all over the world. After we parked on the ramp the captain made the following announcement. "Ladies and gentleman, you must be wondering if all these airplanes around us have the same instrument problem as we have, but the reality is that we are here for a good reason." Then he went on to explain the little bit we knew about the situation in the U.S. There were loud gasps and stares of disbelief.

Bush Addresses the Nation

Because of fears of more attacks, President Bush had kept out of sight for much of the afternoon of September 11. By late afternoon, however, Bush and his advisers decided to return to Washington, D.C., where the Pentagon was still burning. In times of any crisis, Americans have always turned to the president for support, comfort, and leadership. On the evening of September 11, America needed its president to rally the nation. At 8:30 P.M., Bush gave a televised address from the Oval Office in the White House.

George W. Bush's speech
George W. Bush's speech to the nation following the attacks was one of the most important in his presidency. He mourned the losses, reassured the country, and hinted at further action.

Speaking from the Oval Office in the White House, President Bush addresses the nation on the evening of September 11.

Good evening. Today, our fellow citizens, our way of life, our very freedom came under attack in a series of deliberate and deadly terrorist acts. The victims were in airplanes or in their offices—secretaries, businessmen and women, military and **federal** workers. Moms and dads, friends and neighbors.

Thousands of lives were suddenly ended by evil, **despicable** acts of terror. The pictures of airplanes flying into buildings, fires burning, huge structures collapsing have filled us with disbelief, terrible sadness and a quiet, unyielding anger.

These acts of mass murder were intended to frighten our nation into chaos and retreat. But they have failed. Our country is strong. A great people has been moved to defend a great nation. . . .

Today, our nation saw evil, the very worst of human nature, and we responded with the best of America, with the daring of our rescue workers, with the caring for strangers and neighbors who came to give blood and help in any way they could. . . .

This is a day when all Americans from every walk of life unite in our resolve for justice and peace. America has stood down enemies before, and we will do so this time.

None of us will ever forget this day, yet we go forward to defend freedom and all that is good and just in our world.

The Following Days

On September 12, family members and friends of the missing went to Ground Zero in a desperate search. They made **flyers** with pictures of their loved ones and details of their age, weight, height, and any identifying marks. They passed these flyers out to passers-by on the streets. They posted them on lampposts, along subway signs, and on bulletin boards. A church just a short way from Ground Zero was almost covered with these pictures, which formed a wall of grief.

On September 13, in England, the queen ordered a special changing of the guard ceremony outside Buckingham Palace. After the ceremony, the U.S. national anthem was played, followed by two minutes of silence.

On September 14, President Bush attended a service at the National Cathedral in Washington, D.C. He said, "We are here in the middle hour of our grief. So many have suffered so great a loss, and today we express our nation's sorrow. . . . To the children and parents and spouses and families and friends of the lost, we offer the deepest sympathy of the nation. And I assure you, you are not alone."

Leaders of many faiths attended the service. Muzammil H. Siddiqi, a member of the Islamic Society of North America, spoke of "tears and broken hearts." The cathedral's dean, Nathan Baxter, called for restraint. "Let us pray that as we act we not become the evil we deplore," he said.

> **Yesterday was a dark day in the history of humanity, a terrible affront to human dignity.**
> Pope John Paul II

Amanda Ripley's account
Amanda Ripley, a reporter, describes the scene as relatives of the missing arrived at the 69th Regiment Armory on 26th Street, not far from the Empire State Building, to submit information to city workers.

A man holds up a photo of his missing father, who was working on the 96th floor of the north tower on the morning of September 11.

It might be easier to believe the twin towers had been knocked to the ground if people at the 69th Regiment Armory were crying, if they were clinging to one another in tight bunches, filling the gaping auditorium with sobs. But they aren't. Assembled in the hall are thousands of the walking wounded—the hollow-eyed mothers, lovers, brothers of people who went to work two days ago and disappeared. They answer police officers' questions, they hand over dental records, they describe the meaning of obscure [mysterious] tattoos, they feel sick, they tear up [become tearful], they pick at ham sandwiches. But only rarely does someone begin to weep.

Worldwide Reaction

The explosions in New York City and Washington, D.C., brought a huge reaction from around the world. In Canada, Prime Minister Jean Chrétien told a crowd of 75,000, "There will be no silence from Canada. Our friendship has no limit." In England, the queen joined Prime Minister Tony Blair for a service at St. Paul's Cathedral. When the pews filled up with people, thousands more stood outside.

Ireland announced a day of national mourning. Shops and schools closed. In the country's capital, Dublin, a line of people 1 mile (1.6 kilometers) long waited to sign a **condolence book** at the American Embassy. In Paris, France, church bells rang for five minutes, the subway trains were called to a stop, and the elevators at the Eiffel Tower paused.

Albania held a day of national mourning. In Berlin, Germany, up to 200,000 people gathered at the Brandenburg Gate for a ceremony. A banner draped across the gate read "Our Deepest Sympathy" and "We Mourn with You." Germany observed five minutes of silence.

In Russia, the flags were flown at half-mast and flowers were piled at the gate of the American Embassy. Across Europe, everything stopped for three minutes. In South Korea, a minute of silence was begun with the sound of sirens.

Muslims in Pasadena, California, hold a candlelit vigil in memory of the victims of the attacks.

Reactions from around the world
Politicians around the world expressed their personal horror and outrage at the attacks.

As for those that carried out these attacks, there are no adequate words of condemnation. Their barbarism will stand as their shame for all eternity. This mass terrorism is the new evil in our world. . . . We here in Britain stand shoulder to shoulder with our American friends in this hour of tragedy.

Tony Blair, prime minister of Great Britain

This is an act of war by madmen. It is the worst attack on the United States since **Pearl Harbor.** This is one of those few days in life that one can actually say will change everything.

Chris Patten, **European Union** external relations commissioner

The entire international community should unite in the struggle against terrorism. . . . This is a **blatant** challenge to humanity.

Vladimir Putin, president of Russia

This outrageous and vicious act of violence against the United States is unforgivable.

Junichiro Koizumi, prime minister of Japan

The Plot

Even as the World Trade Center and the Pentagon still burned, the top intelligence and security agencies in the United States began investigating who was behind the attacks.

The **terrorists'** plan had been nearly perfect. They had decided to strike on Tuesday, the day of the week when fewest people travel, so there would not be so many passengers to overpower. They had chosen westbound flights, so the planes would be full of fuel. They used **box-cutters** that could be slipped past airport security. Once the terrorists had gained control of the planes, they turned off the device that allowed radar to track the planes precisely.

After checking passenger lists, investigators determined that nineteen hijackers—mostly from Saudi Arabia—had performed the attacks. Later, investigators would discover that many of the hijackers had lived and had trained to fly in the United States. Many of them had families, and they were united in their hatred of America. Their leader was named Osama bin Laden, said U.S. investigators, and their group was called Al Qaeda. Al Qaeda was a shadowy terrorist organization that investigators believed could have followers in countries all over the world.

Bin Laden, at that time, was believed to be in Afghanistan, a war-torn nation in central Asia. He taped a video in the weeks following the attacks that was broadcast on television around the world. He said that because of the attacks, America was filled with fear "from the north to the south and east to west, thank god." Bin Laden had used Afghanistan as a base to train terrorists. The country was then ruled by a group called the Taliban. The United States demanded that the Taliban turn bin Laden over to them.

Osama bin Laden had been shocked when Middle-Eastern countries accepted U.S. help instead of his against the 1990 Iraqi invasion of Kuwait. His Al Qaeda organization was later linked to several attacks against U.S. targets.

Writer Mir Tamim Ansary was born in Afghanistan and lived there until he moved to the U.S. at the age of eighteen. After the September 11 attacks, he wrote an e-mail to some friends: "The only way to get bin Laden is to go in there with ground troops."

Within days, Ansary's e-mail about the September 11 attacks had been forwarded all over the country.

I am from Afghanistan, and even though I've lived here [the United States] for 35 years I've never lost track of what's going on there [Afghanistan]. So I want to tell anyone who will listen how it all looks from where I'm standing.

I speak as one who hates the Taliban and Osama bin Laden. There is no doubt in my mind that these people were responsible for the atrocity in New York and Washington, D.C. I agree that something must be done about those monsters.

But the Taliban and bin Laden are not Afghanistan. They're not even the government of Afghanistan. The Taliban are a **cult** of ignorant **psychotics** who took over Afghanistan in 1997. It's not only that the Afghan people had nothing to do with this atrocity. They were the first victims.

We come now to the question of bombing Afghanistan back to the Stone Age. Trouble is, that's been done. The Soviets took care of it already. Make the Afghans suffer? They're already suffering. Level their houses? Done. Turn their schools into piles of rubble? Done. Eradicate their hospitals? Done. New bombs would only stir the rubble of earlier bombs. The [Taliban] would slip away and hide. So what else is there? The only way to get bin Laden is to go in there with ground troops.

The War against Terror

President Bush carefully avoided using the word "war" in his September 11 speech. But he did challenge the countries of the world to take sides: they were either with the United States or against it.

When the Taliban refused to give up Osama bin Laden, the United States threw its support behind the Northern Alliance, a group of tribes in Afghanistan that opposed the Taliban. American and British **special forces** units began fighting on the ground inside Afghanistan. From the air, American aircraft fired missiles and dropped bombs that smashed the Taliban lines.

By the end of November 2001, the Taliban forces had collapsed and abandoned the capital city, Kabul. In December, a new government took power. American, British, and Afghan forces would continue to find and battle against groups of Al Qaeda forces.

A U.S. special operations soldier smiles as he walks past a boy among crowds of Afghans loyal to the U.S.-backed Northern Alliance.

John Simpson's report

John Simpson, a reporter for the BBC, had filed news reports about the fighting in Afghanistan. He was also among the first journalists in the capital city of Kabul after it was abandoned by the Taliban.

For the BBC team . . . it was an exhilarating moment. Everyone was enormously stirred up and excited. Two people from BBC Radio who **commandeered** bicycles to get to the centre of the city had to give up and take taxis instead; the pressure of the crowd was so great they fell off. After battling my way by foot through a dense mass of people, I also stopped a taxi, and climbed into it with one of my television colleagues. Every time we stopped along the way in order to telephone a report to London, a crowd would gather round us and make talking almost impossible.

A Changed World

On September 11, 2001, the world changed. Final counts indicated that more than 3,000 people were killed in the attacks: 2,792 at the World Trade Center, 184 at the Pentagon, and 40 on Flight 93 in Shanksville, Pennsylvania. The victims were not just from the United States, but from around the world. The fires beneath the wreckage of the twin towers would smolder for months, continuing to fill lower Manhattan with a terrible, burned smell.

The United States, the world's lone **superpower,** found itself at war with a shadowy organization that had formed **cells** around the world. American soldiers were sent to several countries to look for Osama bin Laden and Al Qaeda leaders. Money was also sent to help other countries investigate Al Qaeda within their borders or to improve their security forces.

But Al Qaeda was only the beginning. September 11 completely changed the way the United States viewed the world. Americans had long felt safe from outside conflict, but September 11 shattered that sense of security. The **stock market** was closed. All professional sports games were cancelled for a week. Regular television programming was suspended for round-the-clock coverage of the attacks.

There were other changes. Many had shown heroism during the devastating events of that one day. There was the courage of the passengers on United Airlines Flight 93 and the calmness of cabin staff like Madeline Sweeney. There were those who died in the towers because they refused to leave others who could not walk as well. These acts, along with the many final phone calls of love, left Americans with a stronger sense of national pride and greater willingness to give to others.

Many Americans now believe that America's enemies will not hesitate to bring war to their homes, but President Bush intends to take the war to America's enemies first. His intention has worried both the nation's allies and its enemies. Future historians will judge these events, using the primary sources of September 11.

The *New York Times* article
A day after the attacks, September 12, the lead editorial from the *New York Times* conveys sadness and the sense of a changed world.

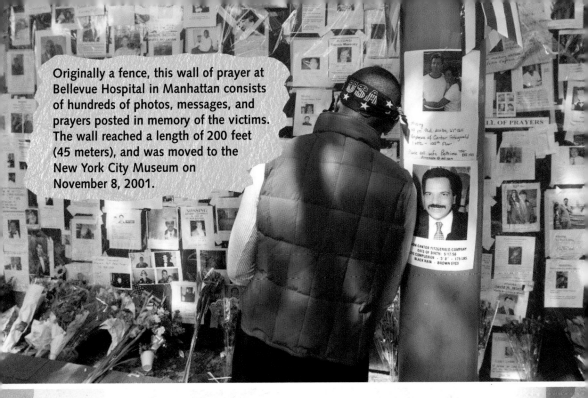

Originally a fence, this wall of prayer at Bellevue Hospital in Manhattan consists of hundreds of photos, messages, and prayers posted in memory of the victims. The wall reached a length of 200 feet (45 meters), and was moved to the New York City Museum on November 8, 2001.

Remember the ordinary, if you can. Remember how normal New York City seemed at sunrise yesterday, as beautiful a morning as ever dawns in early September. . . . All the innumerable habits and routines that define a city were unbroken. Everyone was **preoccupied**, in just the way we usually call innocence.

And by 10:30 A.M. all that had gone. . . . In his evening speech, George W. Bush said yesterday was a day we would never forget. It was, in fact, one of those moments in which history splits, and we define the world as "before" and "after."

We have nearly all had occasion to wonder how civilians who suddenly found their country at war and themselves under attack managed to frame some memory of life as it once was. Now we know. We look back at sunrise yesterday through pillars of smoke and dust, down streets snowed under with the **atomized debris** of the skyline, and we understand that everything has changed.

Timeline

September 11, 2001

8:46 A.M.   American Airlines Flight 11 hits the north tower of the World Trade Center in New York City.

9:03 A.M.   United Airlines Flight 175 hits the south tower of the World Trade Center in New York City.

9:31 A.M.   Bush makes a statement against **terrorism.**

9:39 A.M.   American Airlines Flight 77 hits the Pentagon in Washington, D.C.

9:59 A.M.   The south tower of the World Trade Center collapses.

10:06 A.M.   United Airlines Flight 93 crashes in a field in western Pennsylvania after several passengers call loved ones and say they are going to take back control of the plane.

10:28 A.M.   The north tower of the World Trade Center collapses.

11:45 A.M.   President Bush arrives at Barksdale Air Force Base in Louisiana.

8:30 P.M.   Bush addresses the nation, stating that the world will have to choose between standing with the terrorists or standing with the United States.

Sources for Further Research

Buch, Tonya. *The Crash of United Flight 93 on September 11, 2001.* New York: Rosen Publishing, 2002.

Editorial Staff, Chelsea House Publishers. *America Responds to the Events of September 11, 2001: Call to Rescue, Call to Heal: Emergency Medical Professionals at Ground Zero.* Broomall, Penn.: Chelsea House Publishers, 2003.

Editorial Staff, Raintree Publishers. *September 11, 2001.* Chicago: Raintree Publishers, 2002.

Gard, Carolyn. *The Attack on the Pentagon on September 11, 2001.* New York: Rosen Publishing, 2002.

Gard, Carolyn. *The Attacks on the World Trade Center: February 26, 1993, and September 11, 2001.* New York: Rosen Publishing, 2002.

Stewart, Gail B. *America under Attack: September 11, 2001.* Farmington Hills, Mich.: Gale Group, 2002.

Wheeler, Jill C. *September 11, 2001: The Day That Changed America.* Vaughan, Ontario, Canada: ABDO Publishing Company, 2002.

List of Primary Sources

The author and publisher gratefully acknowledge the following publications and websites from which written sources in the book are drawn. In some cases the wording or sentence structure has been simplified to make the material appropriate for a school readership.

p. 7: Linda Nuñez: Ariel Sharon: http://www.september11news.com/International Reaction.htm

p. 8: Flight Attendant: *New York Daily News*, September 21, 2001, p. 10.

p. 9: Air Traffic Controllers: *New York Times*. October 16, 2001, section B, p. 9.

p. 11: John Labriola: *One Nation: America Remembers September 11*. (Little, Brown and Co., 2001).

p. 13: Bob Borski, Carl Cunneff: *People* magazine, September 24, 2001. "Hell on Earth."
Jim McMahon: CBC news, http://www.cbc.ca/news/indepth/usattacked/diary-mcmahon.html

p. 15: President Bush: *Newsweek*, December 3, 2001. Howard Fineman and Martha Brant: "The Bushes in Wartime: This is Our Life Now."

p. 17: Mike Walter: "Witnesses to the Moments." Porter Anderson, September 11, 2001.
http://www.cnn.com/us

p. 19: Al Jones: "Unspeakable Horror: Eyewitness Accounts of N.Y. Attacks."
http://abcnews.go.com/sections/us/DailyNews/WTC_eyewitness010911.html
M. Corey Goldman: "Terror in the Streets: Morning of Terror and Terrorism Strikes New York City: A Reporter's Notebook." http://abcnews.go.com/sections/business/DailyNews/wtcnotebook_010911.html

p. 21: Stephen King: *New York Times*, January 30, 2002. "Capturing for History Many of a Tragic Day's Triumphs and Problems." Michelle Preli: MSNBC.com staff and wire reports: "Nightmare Scenes in New York City." http://www.msnbc.com/news/627058.asp; John Frey: *People* magazine, September 24, 2001, pp.36-39, "Hell on Earth."

p. 22: Dick Cheney: *Newsweek*, January 7, 2002, "September 11 Stories."
Jere Longman: MSNBC news, *Dateline NBC*, July 30, 2002. http://www.msnbc.com/news/787018.asp

p. 23: Lisa Jefferson: ABC news, interview with Peter Jennings, "World News Tonight." September 21, 2001

p. 24: Yasser Arafat: http://www.september11news.com/International Reaction.htm

p. 25: Regina Wilson: *Women at Ground Zero: Stories of Courage and Compassion*. Susan Hagen and Mary Carouba (Indianapolis: Alpha Books, 2002).

p. 27: Jeff Hinderer, Claudia Brown: *People* magazine, September 24, 2001, p.127, "America Under Attack."

p. 29: Stephen Evans: *The BBC Reports: On America, Its Allies and Enemies, and the Counterattack on Terrorism* (Overlook Press, 2002), p. 29,"Ground Zero."

p. 31: Greg Gulick: *People* magazine, September 24, 2001, p.63, "Crisis Management."

p. 33: President Bush: CBS news, September 11, 2002. "Bush on 9/11: Moment to Moment."
http://www.cbsnews.com/stories/2002/09/10/60IImain521483.html
Lt. Gen. Keck: Associated Press, September 30, 2001. "Officials Recall President as Calm, Down-to-Earth."

p. 34: Rudolf Giuliani: ABC news, September 11, 2001. "In Their Own Words."
http:/www/abcnews.go.com/sections/us/dailynews/wtc-quotes010911.html

p. 35: Craig Childs: National Public Radio, September 18, 2001.

pp. 36–37: Jules Naudet: 9/11 – *The Filmmakers' Commemorative Edition*, Paramount Home Video, 2002.

p. 39: Flight attendant: London Free Press, November 3, 2001, p.F3, "From Despair Comes Hope, Good."

p. 41: President Bush: White House, Office of the Press Secretary, September 11, 2001. "Statement by the President in His Address to the Nation."
http://www.whitehouse.gov/news/releases/2001/09/20010911-16.html

p. 42: Pope John Paul II: http://www.september11news.com/International Reaction.htm

p. 43: Amanda Ripley: *Time* magazine, September 24, 2001, p.77. "The Victims: Facing the End."

p. 45: Tony Blair: BBC news, September 11, 2001. "Blair's Statement in Full."
http://www.bbc.co.uk/2/hi/uk-news/politics/1538551.stm; Chris Patten: BBC news, September 12, 2001.
"World Shock at US Attacks." http://www.bbc.co.uk/2/hi/americas/1537800.stm;
Vladimir Putin: http://www.bbc.co.uk/2/hi/uk-news/politics/1538551.stm

p. 47: Tamim Ansary: *The Record*, September 20, 2001, p.11. "Afghans would gladly be rid of Taliban and Bin Laden."

p. 49: John Simpson: *The BBC Reports: On America, Its Allies and Enemies, and the Counterattack on Terrorism* (Overlook Press, 2002), p. 101. "Afghanistan's Tragedy."

p. 51: *New York Times*, September 12, 2001. "The War Against America, an Unfathomable Attack."

Glossary

affront insult

aide assistant to a military or political figure

articulate to express clearly in words

assassinate to murder a person, usually for a political reason

atomized shattered into tiny pieces

automatic weapon gun that can fire a series of rapid shots

blatant obvious

box-cutter knife used to rip open cardboard boxes. The blade can be retracted.

broker person who buys and sells stock on behalf of others

bunker protected room or series of rooms, usually underground and constructed with extra-strong materials

carnage killing of large numbers of people

cell group of trained terrorists stationed in one place waiting for orders to attack

chaplain priest attached to an army unit or government-run or private organization

char material that has been partially burned and is blackened on the surface

commandeer to take control of something for use in an emergency

commercial having to do with buying and selling; conducted for business reasons

concentric having the same center; one inside the other

condolence book book in which mourners sign their names and express their feelings after a tragedy

cult group whose members gather around a leader or object and follow orders or rules as in a religion

culture set of attitudes about the world and accepted behavior shared by a group and passed from one generation to the next

debris pieces broken off from something that has been damaged or destroyed

dehydrated having insufficient water in one's body

despicable deserving contempt

disoriented unsure where one is and which way one is facing

documentary nonfiction film

European Union group of European countries formed in 1993, which addresses the specific concerns of its member countries

evacuation removing people from an area or building, typically in an emergency

exhort encourage or urge

extremist person who believes deeply in ideas and plans to carry out extreme acts in support of them

federal relating to the U.S. national government based in Washington, D.C.

flyer small leaflet or poster

hub central area

impromptu made up on the spot to deal with a situation

instill introduce (into a person or people) and gradually strengthen

media group of organizations that spread information and entertainment, including television, radio, Internet, and newspapers

pandemonium chaos and panic

paramedic person, not a doctor, trained to give emergency medical treatment

Pearl Harbor location of an unexpected and massively damaging attack on an American naval base in Oahu, Hawaii, by the Japanese in 1941, which provoked the United States into entering World War II

pentagonal in the shape of a pentagon, a geometric figure with five equal sides

preoccupied deep in thought

psychotic insane person

rookie someone who is new or inexperienced

sniper someone who aims and shoots at a person, usually from a hidden position

special forces highly trained soldiers who carry out tasks impossible for ordinary troops

stock market financial center where stocks, shares, and bonds are bought and sold

superpower nation with resources so much greater than those of any, or almost any, other nation, that it dominates world affairs

terrorist person who targets civilians and public spaces to create terror and promote his or her political or religious aims

transcript copy of a conversation that has been written or typed out

veteran person who has experience in a certain area

visibility greatest distance at which large objects can be seen with the naked eye

Index